MW00760915

Authors
Bob Duggan

Product Manager
Maureen Kelly

Editor
John Sprague

Book Design
Barbara Mueller

Cover Design
Karen McDonald

Nihil Obstat
Rev. Msgr. Glenn D. Gardner, J.C.D.

Imprimatur
*Most Rev. Charles V. Grahmann
Bishop of Dallas*

October 15, 1999

The Nihil Obstat and Imprimatur are official declarations that the material reviewed is free of doctrinal or moral error. No implication is contained therein that those granting the Nihil Obstat and Imprimatur agree with the contents, opinions, or statements expressed.

Send all inquiries to:
RCL • Resources for Christian Living
200 Bethany Drive
Allen, Texas 75002-3804

Toll free   800-822-6701
Fax   800-688-8356

Printed in the United States of America

12726   ISBN 0-7829-0977-9

1 2 3 4 5   03 02 01 00 99

Handbook for Neophytes
by Bob Duggan

Introduction

*C*ongratulations! At the Easter Vigil you were "newly planted" (i.e., made a "neophyte") in the Lord. The sacraments of Christian Initiation in which you participated during the "mother of all vigils" have borne fruit in the new life that you now enjoy, a born-again life in Christ, the Risen One.

There is nothing more awesome in our Catholic tradition than what we believe happens in the course of the Easter Vigil. On that night of nights, not only the Church but the world itself is reborn, recreated in grace, through the Christian community's celebration of the paschal mystery. In the glow of the Easter fire, in word and song, in water and oil, in bread and wine, our saving God revisits his people to renew once more the age-old prophecy of a salvation that will never end, to fulfill an ancient promise of a love that has robbed death of its sting once and for all.

Whether your community gathered with you in a grand cathedral or in a makeshift, multipurpose space, whether it was a balmy evening bearing the first hints of spring or a night of bitter cold, whether you were surrounded by hundreds of worshippers whose song was accompanied by a majestic organ or only a handful of the faithful doing their best with guitar and piano, the truth is that you were at the center of the most staggering mystery that the human race will ever enact in sacred sign and symbol.

To unpack the full meaning of what you experienced at the Easter Vigil is the work of a lifetime. Whether you have recognized it or not, the reason the entire Christian community enters into the annual cycle of Lent-Easter each year is because we, too, must spend the rest of our lives exploring the implications of our sacramental immersion into the Christ-event.

In order to help you begin that lifelong process, the Church has set aside a special season, called the Period of Mystagogy, to explore and savor the deeper meanings of what has just happened to you. Throughout the fifty days of the Easter Season, you are invited to use this handbook to probe more and more deeply what it means to be a neophyte, to ponder why—from the very beginning—newly initiated Christians have described themselves as being "born again" in the power of the Holy Spirit.

Even when the fifty days of Easter are completed and the formal Period of Mystagogy has ended, the Church wishes to walk with you in a special way during the first year of your full fellowship with us in the Body of Christ. While this little booklet is meant primarily for your use in the days immediately following your Baptism/Confirmation/ First Eucharist, you may well find it worthwhile to refer back to it from time to time over the coming year. This first year of the "rest of your life" is a special one, and this handbook is meant to help you build on what the catechumenal process has already meant in your life. Share it with your godparent, or use it privately as you see fit. May the Great Fifty Days be for you as a single day of rejoicing in the Lord!

Celebrate
Eucharist

I remember that for weeks after I was baptized, tears would be streaming down my face as I came forward to receive Holy Communion. At first I was embarrassed by this, but pretty soon it just didn't matter. No words could have expressed how much I was feeling as I finally got to take the bread and wine of Holy Communion. Sometimes even now, years later, those tears still come back when I remember how far I've come on my journey since the first day I entered the catechumenate. The Lord has been so terribly, terribly good to me, I just can't get over it.

Delores Rodriguez

For Reflection

▨ Remember the sights and sounds, the tastes and smells of your First Eucharist at the Easter Vigil. Recall the thoughts and feelings that filled you on that night. Jot down some of the images that you will always associate with that evening, and then spend some time prayerfully thanking the Lord for the many, many gifts that have been part of your catechumenal journey.

▨ The Second Vatican Council called the Eucharist the "source and summit" of the Christian life. What do those words mean to you now, in light of your own experience of coming to the eucharistic table?

▨ The Eucharist is also called "Holy Communion." With whom does the Eucharist put you in communion? And what do you think might be some of the deeper implications of being "in communion" with him/her/them?

▨ The "full and active participation" of the faithful at Mass has been described by the bishops at the Second Vatican Council as the "aim above all else" of a renewed liturgical experience. Write down some of your thoughts as to what your own "full and active participation" at Mass will look like in the weeks, months, and years to come.

$\mathcal{F}$or many months, perhaps even for many years, your desire to share in the Eucharist has been growing stronger and stronger. Your yearning to consume the Body of Christ and to drink his Blood have surely been among the clearest of signs to your family and friends, your catechists and other catechumenal team members, that you were indeed ready to be fully initiated at the Easter Vigil this year.

Now that you have been welcomed to the Lord's Table, you will undoubtedly experience the Great Fifty Days of the Easter Season as a time that is intensely eucharistic. Feast on the Lord's Body. Taste the sweetness of his Precious Blood. Delight in the experience of sharing this foretaste of the Heavenly Banquet. Rejoice in the fullness of this communion that we so rightly call "holy."

One of the early Fathers of the Church pointed out that the Eucharist is different from any other kind of nourishment: Every other food that we eat is transformed, he said, and becomes a part of our body. In the case of the Eucharist, however, we are transformed and become what we eat—the Body of Christ. The miraculous conversion of the bread and wine into the Body and Blood of Christ is matched by an equally wondrous transformation: You who once were "far off" are joined now to Christ's Body in a communion as intimate as it is holy.

As you celebrate the fullness of eucharistic communion with us, you should remember that what you receive at the altar not only joins you to the heavenly Christ in a new and deeper way, it also joins you to the members of the Body of Christ here on earth. Your celebration of the Eucharist each Sunday should help you to become increasingly aware of a new solidarity that you enjoy with each and every member of the Church. The Bible often refers to the "fellowship of the saints." Your "fellowship" with other members of your parish and with the Church throughout the world now has sacramental roots that are mysteriously deep and real.

Many centuries ago, newly initiated members would wear their white baptismal robes to church to celebrate Eucharist every day during the Octave of Easter (Easter week) as a way of signaling their importance in the eucharistic assembly. Many communities today still find various ways at the Masses of the Easter Season to show how significant it is that the neophytes are present in the assembly to celebrate Eucharist with them. Some communities have them sit in specially reserved places; others have them carry forward the bread and wine at the preparation of the gifts; still others ask the neophytes to come forward first to receive Communion. Whatever may be the custom in your community, remember that your participation at the eucharistic table is itself a charged symbol of how the Risen Christ is present and working in his Body in every age and place.

Practical Suggestions

- ⚙ If it has not already been arranged for you, ask about how you can carry forward the gifts of bread and wine at the Mass you attend during the Easter Season.

- ⚙ While you were in the catechumenate, you were most likely dismissed from the assembly each week prior to the General Intercessions. Listen now to those prayers in a new way, understanding how the solidarity you enjoy with other members of the Body of Christ creates a new claim on your concern and prayers. Remember to include those same intentions in your prayers throughout the week.

- ⚙ Share with your godparent or someone else close to you what it is like to be able to approach the Lord's Table now with the rest of the assembly. If you keep a journal, be sure to record there the thoughts and feelings this new experience stirs in you.

Savor the Mystery

Every time I attend the Vigil, it's like reliving my baptism all over again. The candles flickering in the darkness send chills down my spine—I can still remember how it took my breath away the first time I saw the light spreading throughout the church as everyone's taper was lit from the Easter Candle. When I go through hard times and it feels like the darkness is really closing in on me, I try to remember that night when it seemed like the light was not just all around me— it was inside me!

Jim Byrne

For Reflection

▨ Think about the water that was used at the Easter
Vigil. You or others were immersed in it, had it
poured on you, or were just sprinkled with it after
the assembly's renewal of baptismal promises. The
prayer of blessing said over the water during the Vigil
speaks of water as a source of both birth and death,
creation and destruction. On the night of the Vigil,
the Church remembers the many ways that water has
been used in the story of salvation as a way of
helping us understand more deeply our own journey
"through the waters." What connections can you
make between God's "holy waters" and your own
faith journey?

▨ Which of the readings that were proclaimed at the
Vigil has "echoed" in your heart most clearly? Why?
What has that reading said to you about the events
unfolding in your life at the present time?

▨ A traditional Catholic hymn speaks of the Holy Spirit's
"sweet anointing from above." What was your experience of the Spirit's anointing in the sacrament of
Confirmation at the Vigil? What did the fragrance of
the chrism suggest to you?

▨ The Risen Christ is alive in his Church in many
different ways. How did you experience his presence
most powerfully during the Vigil? Jot down some of
your reflections on that experience.

When family or friends come over for a visit, newlyweds love to pull out their wedding album and share the photos and memories of their special day. The photos are usually just a jumping-off point for stories that capture the deeper meanings of the wedding day for the couple and those close to them. Something similar happens with neophytes throughout the Easter Season. Each time the community assembles for Eucharist during the Great Fifty Days, the Church "pulls out" images and symbols from the Vigil to stir our memories and to invite us to savor the mysteries that were celebrated in the sacraments of Christian Initiation.

Both the liturgical rituals and the readings that are proclaimed during the Easter Season are filled with echoes of what happened in the darkness of Holy Saturday night, when the Church proclaimed to all the world that Jesus Christ is risen from the dead. Holy water is sprinkled in abundance during this season; the Easter candle burns tall and bright in the sanctuary; and alleluias are sung with gusto. Stories are told of the Risen One, and how the disciples discovered his presence in their midst "in the breaking of the bread" and in the peace that is exchanged as a sign of reconciliation and forgiveness.

In a very special way, this liturgical season is designed just for you—to help you savor the mysteries that are unfolding in your very life, thanks to the sacraments of Baptism, Confirmation, and Eucharist. In one way or another, each and every Sunday celebration during this time is meant to help you "unpack" what it means to have been fully initiated into the Body of Christ at the Easter Vigil. We still have the texts of a number of famous sermons (called "mystagogical catecheses") preached by some of the great bishops of the early Church, in which they explained to the neophytes during this time the full meaning of what happened to them at the Vigil. While your own pastor may not preach with the learning of St. Augustine or the eloquence of St. John Chrysostom, your Sunday celebrations are meant to help you explore the deeper meanings of your "rebirth" in Christ, just as did your predecessors in the ancient catechumenate.

Practical Suggestions

⊛ Look over the coming Sunday's Scripture readings with an eye to recognize how they form a kind of "commentary" on what life in the Risen Christ looks like, either for an individual believer or for the community at large.

⊛ Set aside some quiet time for praying, journaling, or just remembering the richness of the Easter Vigil, and "unpack" for yourself some of the deeper meanings of what has happened to you.

⊛ Make a date to get together with your godparent and/or some other neophytes for some social time. Suggest that everyone bring any photos taken at the Vigil, and relive the excitement of that night as you share your photos.

Do the Works of Love

I've been working at the local soup kitchen for years. But until I was baptized, I never really understood what people meant when they talked about recognizing the face of Christ in the poor. Something happened to me after my baptism—it's hard to put into words—but now I see people who are suffering in a new way.

Kurt Driscoll

For Reflection

▦ No modern-day saint has captured our imaginations quite as powerfully as Mother Teresa of Calcutta. Yet her holiness consisted in very basic acts of compassion toward those who were suffering. If you were to identify the most simple acts of love toward those around you—actions that you could do without heroic measures—what might they be?

▦ Many of the readings from the Acts of the Apostles that are proclaimed during the Easter Season portray the community of disciples as joyfully caring for one another's needs out of a spirit of love. The Christian Scriptures portray such selfless love as a kind of "proof" that the Risen Christ is alive and—through his Spirit—working in the community. What evidences have you seen in your own local community that Christ is alive in those who do the works of love? Can you, in all humility, recognize how his Spirit is working in you, moving you to "do the works of love" in that same joyful spirit shown by the earliest disciples?

▦ If you are already involved in service activity on behalf of the poor and needy, do you have—since your initiation at the Vigil—any new awareness as to the "deeper" meanings of what you are about? Or, if you have not participated regularly in any such activity, might there now be a call to do so? What "difference" does it make in your life to be "born again" in Christ?

One ought not to underestimate the magnitude of the "scandal of the Cross" for the first generation of Christians. Their beloved Jesus, whom they acclaimed as Savior and miracle worker, had died a shameful death as a convicted criminal. Eyewitnesses among them claimed to have seen him risen from the dead, but, following the Ascension, all agreed that he had left them and departed any further earthly existence. If there was no longer the ongoing "proof" of those who were encountering him on a daily basis, how was the Crucifixion to be explained to unbelievers? And how was the community's continued proclamation of his resurrection to be judged credible?

The Acts of the Apostles provides us with a glimpse into how the early disciples resolved this dilemma. They came to recognize the continuing presence of the Risen One in the Spirit that animated their community. In the enthusiastic witness of new converts and especially in "doing the works of love," they recognized how Jesus continued to live in their midst. That is why the author of Acts makes such a point of describing how the "works" of Jesus were being replicated by various members of the community. Peter and John heal a crippled beggar (3:1-10); soon a large number from the towns in the vicinity gather, "bringing the sick and those disturbed by unclean spirits, and they were all cured" (5:16). All in the community shared their material possessions so that the apostles could give "to each according to need" (4:35), and when the Greek-speaking disciples complained that their widows were being neglected, the community immediately took action, selecting Spirit-filled men who were designated as the first deacons (6:1-7).

In the pagan culture of the Roman Empire, the commitment of the Christian community to "do the works of love," even for those not of their number, soon became legendary. Pagan authors are quoted as remarking in amazement, "See how these Christians love one another!" The phrase "Christian charity" became synonymous with a self-sacrificial love for the poor and needy well beyond mere humanitarian concern for one's fellows. "Doing the works of love" in this fashion became, in fact, a theological assertion as well as a "proof" that the Spirit of Jesus lives in the baptized.

This historical perspective may help you appreciate why the *Rite of Christian Initiation of Adults* says that during the Period of Mystagogy neophytes deepen their grasp of the paschal mystery and make it more a part of their lives by ". . . doing the works of charity" (#244). Your participation in acts of love and service during this time remains a living witness (a "proof") that Jesus lives—in you—just as surely as he did in the first community of disciples!

Practical Suggestions

⚘ Talk to someone who is knowledgeable about the full range of service activities in your parish. Familiarize yourself with the many different ways that a Christian community shows its "preferential" love for the poor and powerless. Consider exploring more deeply your own involvement.

⚘ Discuss with your godparent or another neophyte how the Acts of the Apostles "proves" the Resurrection. Connect this to what you witness in your own community, especially among the newly initiated.

⚘ Take a risk by doing some form of charitable service that is a "stretch" for you. If possible, choose something that puts you in immediate contact with those who are suffering. Be sure to spend some time afterward reflecting on whatever happens. See if you can identify how the Spirit was at work in your experience.

Be Realistic

I couldn't believe that the "high" I was on after the Vigil went away so quickly. I really felt terribly empty and like God had deserted me. It made me question whether I really had the faith I thought I had when I so confidently asked to be baptized. But, thank God, it all leveled out eventually, and I realized that every honeymoon comes to an end . . . and that's when "real" love begins!

Kelly Neil

For Reflection

■ Think about a time when you had very unrealistic expectations of a situation or a relationship. How did you react when the "reality" hit you? Now think about what it is that helps you to be more realistic in your expectations of people and situations. Jot down any insights this reflection may offer you as a neophyte.

■ The Period of Mystagogy is often compared to a honeymoon. Play with that image, thinking about how the comparison may have relevance to your own situation right now. Are there any implications this may have for you over the coming months?

■ Discernment of the spiritual gifts that the Spirit has poured out in your heart through the sacraments of Christian Initiation is an important part of the "work" that you as a neophyte are called to do during the Period of Mystagogy. Spend some time thinking about your gifts—especially anything that you sense is "new and different" about you since your initiation. How is God calling you to put those gifts at the service of the Church and the world in which you live? Be realistic, neither under- nor overestimating your gifts, and make some notes here to record your thoughts.

$\mathcal{Y}$our time in the catechumenate was no doubt a very intense period of learning, prayerful introspection, and shared fellowship with other catechumens and candidates. The natural rhythm of such a prolonged experience builds anticipation and usually makes the initiatory experience at the Easter Vigil a memorable highpoint of one's life. However, for some neophytes who have been meeting once or twice a week for many months or even years, the Period of Mystagogy can be something of a "letdown" as the intensity of preparation gives way to a more relaxed pace. This is not always the case, of course, but it should not be a surprise if it happens to you.

Another way in which some neophytes have experienced disillusionment following their initiation has to do with unrealistic expectations about the community at large. The people you have known in the catechumenate are a very special group of parishioners, hand-picked because of their hospitable and supportive way of relating to new members. But in the parish at large, not everyone has the same skills at welcoming. In fact, we are a Church of sinners and we are not all at our best all of the time. So, it is just possible that you may have some negative experiences as your circle of contacts widens within the larger community. Do not let this surprise or discourage you. This is the stuff of life. The "bruising" that sometimes happens to a tender new shoot can be something that strengthens faith.

Yet another way that neophytes sometimes fail to be realistic is by overcommitting themselves to new involvements in the life of the community. A very understandable enthusiasm and desire to "give back" to the community can lead a neophyte to volunteer for far more than he or she is able to do. Especially when frequent catechumenal gatherings are no longer a part of one's routine, it is easy to feel that one has oodles of free time to get involved in committees and ministries. But the *Rite of Christian Initiation of Adults* deliberately characterizes the Period of Mystagogy as a time for deepened reflection and "meditation on the Gospel" just as much as it is a time of activity (#244). Prudence suggests that, at least at the outset, "less is more" for most neophytes, and careful discernment ought to take place prior to taking on any new, ongoing commitments.

Practical Suggestions

⚬ The *Rite of Christian Initiation of Adults* says that neophytes "should experience a full and joyful welcome into the community" (#246), and it admonishes the faithful to "give them thoughtful and friendly help" (#244). As a neophyte you also need to be open to seek out new relationships beyond the confines of the catechumenal community. During the Easter Season, take the initiative to meet one new person each time you come to Mass.

⚬ Ask God in prayer to show you how you are called to live differently in light of your full initiation into the Body of Christ. Try to identify one new involvement that you feel attracted to, and find out more information about it. Talk to someone who will give you honest feedback about whether or not you should make such a commitment.

⚬ After the many demands of the catechumenate that kept you so busy during Lent, you probably need a "break" of some sort. Figure out a way that you can give yourself (and your family) a treat by just relaxing and having fun. Italians have an expression, *"il dolce far niente"* ("sweet do-nothing") that captures a profound truth about the need for leisure as the basis of true celebration. Give yourself permission to celebrate in that way during this Easter Season!

Stay Connected

I guess I just didn't appreciate how much our catechumenate group had "spoon-fed" me for so long. When I didn't have the group to go to every Sunday, I just couldn't find my niche. I didn't know how to connect in such a big parish, and for a while I just dropped out. Luckily, my sponsor just wouldn't let me drift off, and he gave me a good talking to about how I had to be responsible for my own spiritual welfare.

Valerie Laurel

For Reflection

 Look back over your life and call to mind how you have handled long-term commitments in the past. Recognize the patterns that fostered and supported honoring those commitments. In the same way, see if there are any habits in your life that work against perseverance. What do you need to "flourish" as a practicing Catholic for the rest of your life?

 The American spirit of rugged individualism and privatism is pervasive and influential, even in the religious sphere. Your catechumenal journey was strongly and deliberately communal and public. This was done so that you would understand that faith is social and communal, every bit as much as it is private and individual. Make a list of some of the ways that your understanding of faith still shows the influence of American culture more than the theology of Roman Catholicism.

 Think about the relationships in your life that have been most nourishing and supportive—the ones that have made you who you are today. Ponder how important it was that you "stay connected" to those relationships in order for them to have exercised such a strong formative influence on you. Consider how staying closely connected to the community of believers in the Catholic Church is of the essence to shape and support your growth in faith.

*C*atechumenate team members across the country report that all too often neophytes "disappear" after their initiation at the Vigil. Sometimes it's just a matter of the new members not returning for the formal sessions that have been planned for them during the Easter Season. Other times, and more seriously, what is reported is that the neophytes never really connect with the larger community after their initiation and gradually cease coming even to Sunday Eucharist.

The reasons for this phenomenon are varied and somewhat difficult to ascertain. When it is a question of not coming back to sessions offered during the Easter Season, the reason most frequently suggested is "burnout." That is, neophytes are so exhausted from the demands made on them during Lent, that they just can't bear the thought of leaving home for one more meeting. In the case of those who fall away completely from the practice of their new faith, one of the explanations most frequently voiced is that they were too sheltered in the supportive environment of the catechumenate and consequently were unprepared to sustain their commitment in the "real world" of everyday Catholicism. Another suggestion is that their progress through the catechumenate had been too rapid, that deep conversion and catechesis had not taken place, and that as a result a lifetime commitment to the Catholic Church had not had time to mature.

As a neophyte yourself, what are your thoughts on this matter? More importantly, how do you plan on *not* becoming one of these statistics? Staying connected to your parish community is not a matter of casual importance for the survival of your new faith. It is your lifeline, and the single most important way of avoiding the sad possibility of losing what you have looked forward to for so long. In chapters 12 through 15 of 1 Corinthians, Paul uses the image of a body and its parts to indicate the vital link of the individual believer with the larger Church community. To cut oneself off from the body of the

Church was, for Paul, the death of faith. Paul was a realist about the struggles that membership in the community involves. But for him it was unthinkable for one's faith in Christ to survive apart from the Church, her preaching of the Word, her celebration of the sacraments, and her life of charity. As a neophyte—newly planted— perhaps the most important words of this little booklet are the two at the top of this chapter: Stay Connected!

Practical Suggestions

⊛ Read chapters 12 through 15 of St. Paul's First Letter to the Corinthians, and try to appreciate the struggle for faith in that community. Try to gain an apprecition of how important it was for the apostle and his disciples in Corinth to be "connected" to the Church as the only way that they could remain living "in Christ." Find someone—your godparent or spouse or one of your catechists—and discuss your insights and their implications for your own situation as a neophyte.

⊛ Make certain that you know where and when the sessions are planned for neophytes, both during the Easter Season and throughout the year. Mark them on your calendar and take whatever steps will guarantee that you are able to participate faithfully.

⊛ Don't wait for the catechumenate team to make all of the arrangements for you to stay connected to the other neophytes and to the community at large. Take responsibility yourself for remaining in touch with those who have supported your faith journey to this point.

⊛ Have a talk with your godparent about how you see yourself "connecting" to the parish in the months and years ahead. Be honest and practical.

Offer Witness

When I first joined the pre-catechumenate, I hated the thought of standing up in front of everyone for the rites. I swore they'd never get me to speak in public like some of the others I'd seen. But I feel so full of love now, and so grateful, that I just wanted to "give back" for all I've gotten. When the director of our catechumenate asked if I'd speak at one of the Masses, I just said "YES" without hesitation. It didn't keep my legs from shaking when I got up to speak, but I'm glad I did. Maybe that's what they mean by the "power of the Holy Spirit."

Nicholas O'Neill

For Reflection

※ Think about times when you were "turned off" by the way someone tried to share their faith or religious views with you. What was it that most disturbed you? Jot down here some of the things you want to avoid whenever you share your faith with others.

※ Now remember people whose words or example witnessed powerfully to you about the message of the Gospel. Try to identify what it was about them that you found most attractive. Write down some of the qualities you would like to imitate in your own attempts to share the Good News of God's love with others.

※ Make a list of the unchurched people you know who would most profit from sharing what you have found in the Catholic Church. Think about ways that you might subtly or even explicitly "invite" some of them to explore more deeply their own spiritual journey.

※ What are the things that are most likely to block you from being an effective evangelizer? How might you overcome those obstacles? Write down your thoughts.

*I*n his Apostolic Letter on *Evangelization in the Modern World,* Pope Paul VI says that "the test of truth, the touchstone of evangelization" happens when "the person who has been evangelized goes on to evangelize others." It is "unthinkable," the Pope adds, "that a person should accept the Word and give himself to the kingdom without becoming a person who bears witness to it and proclaims it in his turn" (#24). The significance of these words for every neophyte should be obvious.

You have come to full faith in Christ and his Church, thanks to those who have evangelized and catechized you. Now, fully initiated, you in turn must pass on to others the Good News which first attracted you to the Church. In the strongest possible terms, the Holy Father makes it clear that this is not an optional element for a Christian. Evangelization—giving witness to one's faith—lies at the heart of what it means to be a believer. Evangelization, the Pope teaches, is the very reason for the Church's existence; it is her "deepest identity" (#14).

It is helpful to remember that the Holy Father explains that there are many different ways to evangelize. The "wordless witness" (#21) of a life lived in love and service of others is itself a kind of first proclamation of the Gospel. But it is insufficient to remain at the level of a "wordless witness." We must also be ready, as the First Letter of Peter admonishes us, "to give an explanation to anyone who asks you for a reason for your hope" (1 Peter 3:15). As one who has only recently been "born again" in the new life of baptism and/or has just begun to feast at the Table of the Lord, your enthusiasm and joy over participating in the Church's sacramental life will certainly raise questions in the minds of many who do not share our Catholic Faith. The Period of Mystagogy is a time ripe with opportunities for you to share your faith, to give public witness to the "difference" that Christ has made in your life.

You may be asked to speak about your experience in the catechumenate at one of the Masses during the

Easter Season, or to a group in the parish in a less formal setting. Or your opportunity to give witness may be more spontaneous, as situations arise at work or in social settings among your friends and acquaintances. Never underestimate, either, the power of sharing your experience with family members who still may not fully understand your decision to become Catholic. Be alert to the opportunities that present themselves during this time and in the future to witness to your faith. In doing so, you are engaging in one of the most fundamental tasks that a Christian has been empowered by the Spirit to perform. You are "just beginning" to practice skills that are your God-given charisms, gifts meant for the Church and for the world, to bring the Good News of God's love to more and more of God's children.

Practical Suggestions

◉ If no one has yet asked you to do so, approach a member of the catechumenate team and inquire where and how you might be allowed to share with others your experience in the catechumenate.

◉ Read the stories in the Acts of the Apostles that describe how fearlessly the first disciples shared their faith, even in the face of violent opposition. Talk to your godparent about any fears you may feel at the prospect of giving public witness to your faith.

◉ If public speaking is difficult for you, consider alternative ways that you may be able to share your enthusiasm for the Gospel with others. For example, you might write a letter to your diocesan newspaper about your experience at the Vigil. Or to the secular press about an issue currently in the news, sharing your views and tying them directly into your perspective as a person of Catholic Christian faith.

Act like a Neophyte

Immediately after my baptism, I was so eager to be considered an "insider." It seemed like forever that I had been waiting to be allowed to take the sacraments. I didn't even want anyone to think of me as a neophyte, a beginner. I just wanted to blend into the parish. But looking back on that first year now, I realize what an important time of growth it really was. I thought I was "finished" when I was baptized. But I quickly discovered how much more growing I still had to do. Thank God for my godmother who kept challenging me!

Joseph Uniacke

For Reflection

⊞ Spend some time remembering all of the ways that you have changed since you first entered the pre-catechumenate. Write down the most important areas of growth that you have experienced as part of your spiritual journey in the catechumenate.

⊞ Now think about where you want to be spiritually one year from now. Be as concrete and specific as you can, and then make a list of the spiritual goals you want to set for yourself.

⊞ Try to remember other times in your life when you were a "newcomer" or a "beginner" at something. Did you learn any lessons about how to proceed in such situations that will help you now as a neophyte? Jot down those "lessons learned" for future reference.

$\mathcal{A}$nthropologists who have made cross-cultural studies of "rites of passage" have observed that even after the final ritual celebrations marking a person's change of status, there is generally a transitional time when that person (and the community) become accustomed to the individual's new identity. The Period of Mystagogy is just such a transitional time. You are now fully initiated into the Roman Catholic Church, yet it is "natural" for you to need some time to become accustomed to the "new person" you have become in Christ.

Allow yourself to take that time, to make good use of the "permission" you have been given by the Church to be a "newcomer" for a while longer yet. Act like the neophyte that you are, and do not feel that you must suddenly "have it all together" as much as lifelong Catholics. Enjoy the newness and the freshness of your experience of the sacraments. Delight in the keen appreciation that comes only from one's "first encounters" with so many aspects of sharing the Body and Blood of the Lord. Ask questions, and give others the opportunity to share their own experiences with you. Do not take on too much, as if your faith were mature and tested. Remember how St. Paul told his disciples at Corinth, "I fed you milk, not solid food, because you were not able to take it. Indeed, you are still not able, even now" (1 Corinthians 3:2).

Give yourself plenty of time to integrate all that has happened to you at the Vigil and in the days and weeks since then. Chew on those memories for a while longer yet, savoring their deeper meanings and allowing their significance to dawn on you gradually and ever more completely. Don't be in a rush to "get on with it" and act as if you've been a Catholic forever. Rather, make a point of enjoying your status as a neophyte, newly planted, for the full year prescribed. It is meant to be a time of special pastoral care for you by your community and especially your catechumenate team.

Practical Suggestions

⊛ Listen to how the Church, in the *Rite of Christian Initiation of Adults* (#244-247), describes what this time should be like for you:

- a time for the community and the neophytes to grow together
- deepening their grasp of the paschal mystery
- making [the paschal mystery] part of their lives
- meditation on the Gospel
- sharing in the Eucharist
- doing the works of charity
- a fuller and more effective understanding of the mysteries
- a new perception of the faith, of the Church, and of the world
- a full and joyful welcome into the community
- closer ties with the other faithful
- new, personal experience of the sacraments and of the community

⊛ Surely, to capture all of this richness, a full year is not too much time. Act like a neophyte, with all of the exuberance and joy that being "born again" deserves. Your experience, the **Rite** states, "has an impact on the experience of the community" (#246). Do not deprive us of the opportunity to see the world of grace in all of its freshness through your eyes. Act like a neophyte, that we the faithful might glimpse once again the wonder of God's grace, poured out on us with lavish love in sign and symbol, word and sacrament. Act like a neophyte, so that the community at large might learn again how to appreciate the awe-inspiring mysteries that celebrate our salvation.

ADVICE TO NEOPHYTES

During the fourth and fifth centuries, bishops who were both pastors and theologians instructed the newly baptized during sermons (called mystagogical catecheses) they preached at the Masses of Easter week. Here are excerpts from some of those homiletic instructions.

"So when you come forward [to receive communion], do not come with arm extended or fingers parted. Make your left hand a throne for your right, since your right hand is about to welcome a king. Cup your palm and receive in it Christ's body, saying in response *Amen* . . . After partaking of Christ's body, go to receive the chalice of his blood. Do not stretch out your hands for it. Bow your head and say *Amen* to show your homage and reverence, and sanctify yourself by partaking also of Christ's blood . . . Maintain these traditions without stain, and keep yourselves free from faults. Do not cut yourselves off from communion, do not deprive yourselves of these holy and spiritual mysteries through stain of sins."—Cyril of Jerusalem

"Through the sacrament of baptism you are dead to the old enticements of sin and have risen again through the grace of Christ. This is a death, then, not in the reality of bodily death, but in likeness. When you are immersed, you receive the likeness of death and burial, you receive the sacrament of his cross; because Christ hung on the cross and his body was fastened to it by the nails. So you are crucified with him, you are fastened to Christ, you are fastened by the nails of our Lord Jesus Christ lest the devil pull you away."—Saint Ambrose

"Therefore we should approach priests with great confidence and reveal to them our sins. With the greatest care, compassion and charity they treat sinners according to the rules I have already explained to you. They will not make public anything that should not be revealed, but keep to themselves the sins that have been committed; for like true, watchful fathers, they must respect their sons' sense of shame when they impose upon their sons' bodies the treatment that will cure them. In this way, by putting our lives in order, by recognizing the greatness of the mysteries, that invaluable gift to which we had been invited and which will put us in debt all our lives long, and by taking due care to correct